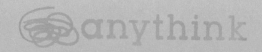

SCIENCE
in Action
MY SENSES

TASTE

Sally Hewitt

This library edition published in 2016 by
Quarto Library., an imprint of QEB Publishing, Inc.

6 Orchard, Lake Forest, CA 92630

Distributed in the United States and Canada by
Lerner Publisher Services
241 First Avenue North
Minneapolis, MN 55401 U.S.A.
www.lernerbooks.com

A CIP record for the book is available from the
Library of Congress.

ISBN 978 1 60992 884 1

Printed in China

Publisher: Maxime Boucknooghe
Editorial Director: Victoria Garrard
Art Director: Miranda Snow
Series Editor: Claudia Martin
Series Designer: Bruce Marshall
Photographer: Michael Wicks
Consultant: Kristina Routh

The author and publisher would like to thank
Sam, Georgina, Millie, Emily, and Lakia.

Words in **bold** can be
found in the glossary
on page 22.

Contents

Taste this!

You have five main senses that give you information about the world around you.

The fives senses are taste, touch, smell, sight, and hearing. This book is about taste.

Your sense of taste tells you about what you eat and drink.

Everything you eat has its own taste. Some things you like, and some things you dislike. If you have eaten something before, your brain will remember it.

Have you tasted any of these foods?

Lemon

Apples

Can you describe what they taste like?

Write down a list of words that you can use to describe different tastes.

Pepper

Carrot

Your taste

You usually choose food because you like the taste of it.

What is your favorite food? Why do you enjoy it so much?

What is your least favorite food? Why don't you like it?

◀ Do you like trying food you have never eaten before?

Activity

Not everyone likes the same tastes.

- Ask your family and friends which of these foods they like.

Tick the boxes, like this:

	Love	Like	Don't like
Broccoli		✔ ✔	✔
Chocolate	✔ ✔ ✔		
Banana	✔	✔	✔
Spicy curry	✔	✔ ✔	

- Count the ticks. Which is the most popular food? What does it taste like?

Stick out your tongue

Your tongue is the part of your body you taste with. It is covered in tiny **taste buds**.

Your taste buds can pick up on five basic tastes: **sweet, salty, sour, bitter,** and **umami**. Umami is a savory, meaty taste.

Does my ice cream taste sweet or umami?

Taste buds tell your brain what you are eating.

When food tastes sweet, such as honey, you may want to eat more.

MMMM

▲ If food tastes bitter, you might want to spit it out!

Find the flavor

Some food doesn't taste very strong. It doesn't have much flavor.

Some people like to change the flavor of their food by adding strong-tasting sauces like tomato ketchup or spices like pepper.

This needs pepper!

Activity

Some flavors taste delicious together, but others taste strange.

Try this test to see which flavors make food taste better or worse.

- Add a little bit of each of these flavors—pepper, jam, lemon juice, and ketchup—to pieces of chocolate, apple, carrot, and bread.

- Which flavors do you think taste good together? Which taste horrible?

Taste and smell

Smell and taste work together to help you enjoy your food. A delicious smell tells your brain that the food will taste good!

When you have a cold and can't smell very well, your food doesn't taste as strong as usual.

This smells good.

Activity

You use your senses of smell and sight, as well as your sense of taste, to tell you what you are eating.

- Ask a friend to shut his or her eyes and hold their nose while they eat small pieces of...

Orange

Radish

Doughnut

Cheese

- Can your friend tell you what the food is just by the taste? Does smelling the food make it taste stronger?

Mouth watering

When you are about to eat your favorite food, do you feel your mouth water? The "water" in your mouth is called **saliva**.

Sometimes just the smell of food makes your mouth water!

◀ Saliva makes your food easier to swallow.

Saliva starts to break down your food so your body can **digest** it. Saliva turns the **starch** in bread into sugars that your body can use more easily.

▲ Chew a piece of bread for a long time. Does it start to taste sweet?

Saliva carries the taste of your food into your taste buds.

◀ Do you have to chew a lollipop to taste it?

Fresh and tasty

Fresh food looks and smells delicious. You want to eat it!

The date on packaged food helps you to know how fresh it is.

After that date, the food starts to go bad or **stale** and will not taste so good.

Old and stale food doesn't look good. It smells awful and tastes terrible!

You don't want to eat it!

The look, smell, and taste warn you: "This food isn't fresh!"

▶ Old fruit and vegetables are good for compost. Compost helps your plants grow in the garden.

Tasting colors

The color of food helps us to imagine what it might taste like.

What do you expect green food to taste like?

Color helps us choose whether the food we eat is safe.

◀ Would you like to eat this food?

Activity

Strange-colored food makes you think it will taste strange, too!

- Draw food you like to eat. Give it colors and patterns, like the apples in this picture.

- Ask your friends what it might taste like.

- Would they like to eat it?

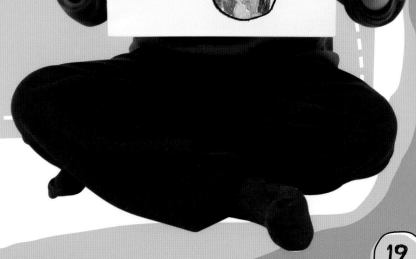

19

New tastes

In stores, you can buy different food from around the world.

▲ Chillies and spices make curry hot and tasty.

There are all kinds of flavors you may not have tasted before. Try them. You might like them!

Activity

With an adult's help, try adding new flavors to your food.

- Put a different vegetable in your soup or add a pinch of herbs.

- Put a new fruit into your fruit salad and add a drop of vanilla essence.

- If you have spices in your pantry, give them a sniff. Which spice could you add to pasta or stew?

- What new flavor could you add to your pizza?

GLOSSARY

Bitter

Dark chocolate often tastes bitter.

Digest

When your body digests food, it mashes it up, uses the goodness, and gets rid of the waste.

Saliva

Saliva is the spit in your mouth. It helps you to taste and swallow food.

Salty

When food tastes of salt, it is salty.

Sour

Lemon tastes sour.

Stale

Stale food is old. It is starting to dry out and smell.

Starch

Starch is found in potatoes, bread, and rice. Your body turns starch into energy.

Sweet

Sugar tastes sweet.

Taste buds

Tiny bumps on your tongue which tell you if your food tastes sweet, sour, salty, bitter, or umami.

Umami

Umami is a savory (meaty) taste. Foods that taste strongly umami are meat, fish, mushrooms, and ripe tomatoes.

INDEX

NEXT STEPS

Teacher safety note:
If you are having a tasting at school, ask each child to bring a letter from home telling you of any food allergies or confirming the child has none.

❋ Encourage children to predict the taste of foods. Will the apple taste sweet or sour? How will lemon juice make the apple taste? Will it be a nice taste?

❋ Find words about taste throughout the book, such as flavor, sweet, sour, bitter, salty, and umami. Talk about how different foods taste using these words. You could write poems or stories using these words.

❋ Create your own 'Taste Tables'. Collect drawings and photographs of food for each of the taste groups—sweet, sour, salty, bitter, and umami. Stick the pictures onto five large sheets of paper. Are there any similarities between the foods? For example, are all the sweet foods fruit?

❋ Talk about food hygiene and safety. Never taste unfamiliar food, berries, or nuts without first checking with an adult. Always wash your hands before handling food. Make sure food is clean, fresh, or well-cooked before tasting it.

❋ Make a collage of your favorite meal using cut-out pictures or drawings. Each meal must have at least one food from each of the taste groups, for example, a flavoring, such as lemon for sour. Label all the foods with one of the taste groups.

❋ When you go to the store, talk about the food you buy. Discuss the tastes you like and don't like. Choose an unfamiliar food and talk about what it might taste like. Prepare and eat it together.